CHANGEABLE THUNDER

BOOKS BY DAVID BAKER

POETRY

Changeable Thunder (2001)
The Truth about Small Towns (1998)
After the Reunion (1994)
Sweet Home, Saturday Night (1991)
Haunts (1985)
Laws of the Land (1981)

CRITICISM

Heresy and the Ideal: On Contemporary Poetry (2000)
Meter in English: A Critical Engagement (1996)

CHANGEABLE THUNDER

POEMS BY

DAVID BAKER

THE UNIVERSITY OF ARKANSAS PRESS

FAYETTEVILLE

2001

09   08   07   06   05   7   6   5   4   3

Designed by Ellen Beeler

Library of Congress Cataloging-in-Publication Data

Baker, David, 1954–
    Changeable thunder : poems / by David Baker.
        p. cm.
    ISBN 1-55728-715-5 (pbk. : alk. paper)
    I. Title.
    PS3552.A4116 C48 2001
    811'.54—dc21
                                                2001003103

for Ann and Kate

ACKNOWLEDGMENTS

These poems have appeared in the following magazines, to whose editors I extend my grateful acknowledgment: *Arts & Letters,* "Two Clouds"; *The Atlantic Monthly,* "After Rain"; *Chelsea,* "Début de Siècle"; *The Colorado Review,* "That Moon"; *Crazyhorse,* "To Winter"; *Five Points,* "Mr. Whitman's Book," "Separation"; *The Georgia Review,* "Midwest: Ode," "Simonides' Stone"; *The Gettysburg Review,* "Cold Water," "Dejection," "Postmodernism"; *The Midwest Quarterly,* "Humble House"; *The Missouri Review,* "'Fade-Out': A Lover's Discourse"; *The North American Review,* "Pulp Fiction"; *The Paris Review,* "Forced Bloom"; *Ploughshares,* "Works and Days"; *Poetry,* "Ohio Fields after Rain"; *The Progressive,* "Midwest: Georgics"; *Raritan,* "Preparatory Meditation," "The Puritan Way of Death," "The Rainbow," "Romanticism"; *The Southern Review,* "The City of God," "Trees beside Water"; *The Southwest Review,* "Unconditional Election"; *The Yale Review,* "Benton's Clouds."

I am very grateful to the John Simon Guggenheim Memorial Foundation, the Ohio Arts Council, and Denison University for their generous support as I worked on this book.

CONTENTS

ONE

TWO

THREE

ONE

*In a single moment of time
Many are the winds that blow this way and that.*

—Pindar

BENTON'S CLOUDS

The background is clouds and clouds above those
the color of an exhaustion, whether
of field hands stacking sheaves, or the coiling,
columnar exhaust of a coal engine.

It is eighteen seventy in nineteen
twenty-seven in nineteen ninety-eight.
The colors of his clouds express each new
or brooding effluence felt elsewhere as

progress, no matter which foreground story,
no matter the gandy dancer contoured
as corn field, no matter Persephone
naked as herself, as a sinew of

rock ledge or oak root yet pornographic
under the modern elder leering down.
The background is everywhere telling.
In the present moment, in the real air,

what we saw above the lake was an art—
gulls and then no gulls, swirl of vacation
debris twirling in funnels from the pier
though the wind rushed in wilder off the surge,

clouds, then not clouds but a green-gray progress
of violences in the lowing air, waves
like a bad blow under water. We stood
at the pier railing and watched it come on.

It is too late to behold the future,
if by future what we mean is the passed-
over detail in the painting which tells
where the scene is destined to lead—Benton's

brilliance, beside the roiling billowy
cloud banks blackened as battlefield debris,
beside the shapely physique of nature
on the move, its machinery of change,

is history in an instant. How else
infuse his Reconstruction pastorals,
his dreamy midwifes, sod farmers, dancing
hay bales wrapped in billows of sallow light,

with an agony befitting the some-
time expatriate Modernist Wobbly
harmonica player he was. Who else
could execute such a beautiful storm,

whipped white, first a color on the water
like a wing or natural improvement.
When the Coast Guard boat swept by us waving,
it was already too late and too close.

The storm took down the big tree in seconds.
Though we were running, swirl of muscle, bales
and billows of fear like the wind breaking
over each swell with the force of a hand,

though we cleared the first breakwall and elm grove,
it was only accident the baby's
carriage was not crushed by the linden bough
sheared off, clean as a stick. We were standing

in the grinding rain, too soon still for tears.
It was too soon to tell what damages
there would be, though we knew, as in his art,
as though before the last skier had tipped

into the lake, there was peril ahead.
We could see it all in an instant's clear
likeness, where the future is not coming
but is already part of the story.

PULP FICTION

You want more? You want some more of this *shit?*
so he puts his weight to his elbow jammed
under the jaw of the other one pinned
there, panicked, panting, his back to the bricks.
The others are loud and jeering and stand
in a jackal circle a spitting-length
away. The cold air is full of bird song.

The sex—sheer sugar—of the flowering trees
turns to powder against the skin, and cakes
the sidewalks pale green, and packs the curbs.
Far away a powerful siren cries.
Someone is about to get his ass kicked.
But now the cruel gang spots someone—okay,
it's me—who is writing this whole scene down.

It's so easy to surpass the limits
of the powers of description. *What are*
you *looking at?* There are yellow flowers
sprouting from the downspout above their heads.
The powers of discursion are no less
feeble, frail as the least petal. *Stop it!*
They don't stop it. The one in trouble is

starting to weep, and the others to laugh,
as the one with the elbow suddenly
slips a white-handled knife from his pocket.
(Is this the big city? Are there dime bags
dropping from the claws of carrion birds?
Have his bad colors taunted the wrong turf?)
No. No. No. This is just my little town,

and the hostile gang is as easily
eight-years-old as twenty, out of grade school
since three o'clock. I'm sorry for my mind,
but the spring has spread a violent seed
and it has taken root in this poem,
as in my heart, in the children beating
each other to a pulp in your city

as well as mine. Is it less barbarous
to turn now toward the beautiful? Once
there was a hillside of white, wild lilies.
The mayapples were spilling there. A first
green froth of spring ferns spread under the pines—
so the pastoral, unperturbed lilies
stand around our absence in the sunlight.

What have we done to deserve the pollen,
the plant persistence of our natures? You
want more? The boys beat the daylights out of
the poor boy and I do nothing to help.

And the flowers are fiction—descriptive,
discursive—designed to suggest my mind
in peace or shame. So are the boys, if

the truth be told. So are the sexual trees.
The knife, you understand, is real. The knife is mine.

FORCED BLOOM

1.

Such pleasure one needs to make for oneself.
She has snipped the paltry forsythia
to force the bloom, has cut each stem on
the slant and sprinkled brown sugar in a vase,
so the wintered reeds will take their water.
It hurts her to do this but she does it.
When are we most ourselves, and when the least?
Last night, the man in the recessed doorway,
homeless or searching for something, or sought—
all he needed was one hand and quiet.
The city around him was one small room.
He leaned into the dark portal, gray
shade in a door, a shadow of himself.
His eyes were closed. His rhythm became him.
So we have shut our eyes, as dead or as
other, and held the thought of another
whose pleasure is need, face over a face . . .

2.

It hurts her to use her hands, to hold
a cup or bud or touch a thing. The doctors

have turned her burning hands in their hands.

The tests have shown a problem, but no cause,

a neuropathology of mere touch.

We have all made love in the dark, small room

of such need, without shame, to our comfort,

our compulsion. I know I have. She has.

We have held or helped each other, sometimes

watching from the doorway of a warm house

where candletips of new growth light the walls,

the city in likeness beyond, our hands

on the swollen damp branch or bud or cup.

Sometimes we are most ourselves when we are

least, or hurt, or lost, face over a face—.

You have, too. It's your secret, your delight.

You smell the wild scent all day on your hand.

ROMANTICISM

It is to Emerson I have turned now,
damp February, for he has written
of the moral harmony of nature.
The key to every man is his thought.
But Emerson, half angel, suffers his
dear Ellen's dying only half-consoled
that her lungs shall no more be torn nor her

head scalded by her blood, nor her whole life
suffer from the warfare between the force
& delicacy of her soul & the
weakness of her frame . . . March the 29th,
1832, of an evening strange
with dreaming, he scribbles, I visited
Ellen's tomb & opened the coffin.

—Emerson looking in, clutching his key.
Months of hard freeze have ruptured the wild
fields of Ohio, and burdock is standing
as if stunned by persistent cold wind
or leaning over, as from rough breath.
I have brought my little one, bundled and
gloved, to the lonely place to let her run,

hoary whiskers, wild fescue, cracks widened
along the ground hard from a winter drought.
I have come out for the first time in weeks
still full of fever, insomnia-fogged,
to track her flags of breath where she's dying
to vanish on the hillsides of bramble
and burr. The seasonal birds—scruff cardinal,

one or two sparrows, something with yellow—
scatter in small explosions of ice.
Emerson, gentle mourner, would be pleased
by the physical crunch of the ground, damp
from the melt, shaped by the shape of his boot,
that half of him who loved the Dunscore heath
too rocky to cultivate, covered thick

with heather, gnarled hawthorn, the yellow furze
not far from Carlyle's homestead where they strolled,
—that half of him for whom nature was thought.
Kate has found things to deepen her horror
for evenings to come, a deer carcass tunneled
by slugs, drilled, and abandoned, a bundle
of bone shards, hoof and hide, hidden by thick

bramble, or the bramble itself enough
to collapse her dreams, braided like rope, blood-
colored, blood-barbed, tangled as Medusa.

What does she see when she looks at such things?
I do not know what is so wrong with me
that my body has erupted, system
by system, sick unto itself. I do

not know what I have done, nor what she thinks
when she turns toward her ill father. How did
Emerson behold of his Ellen, un-
embalmed face fallen in, of her white hands?
Dreams & beasts are two keys by which we are
to find out the secrets of our own natures.
Half angel, Emerson wrestles all night

with his journal, the awful natural
fact of Ellen's death, which must have been
deeper sacrifice than a sacrament.
Where has she gone now, whose laughter comes down
like light snow on the beautiful hills?
Perhaps it is the world that is the matter . . .
—His other half worried by the wording.

TREES BESIDE WATER

1.

                    Stag-
headed elders, the book
calls them, trash trees.

The protrusive is
what the eye draws to—
not the canopy of leaves

but their stripped
limbs sticking through.
This makes the elders

seem stunted beside
the pond sycamores.
To waken, not having

slept, is to find
oneself on the other
side of the shore.

2.

For months I lie down
in a fever. When I
look out, as over

landscape, when my night
fills with brambles—
the rope, the blood-braid

of the briar rose
spreading a dark shore—
I feel the veins of

my body looping
with poison, ripened
with lymph. I lie down

in the night, and my
tree swells within me,
jagged, wild, thorned.

3.

And so the sky fills—
so my limbs shudder,
as on a breeze, when

something with claws lifts
and lands again down
the length of the shore.

What commerce is a
breeze, which our elders
called "an ether, so

fine a liquid one
might sail there," as clouds
of stars rinse from the

sky like waste, water,
fever of leaves on
an eddy of sweat.

4.

Sometimes I cry out
and no one hears me.
Sometimes, even now,

I can't tell the trees
from a force in the
wind or the words

in a book. And my
night goes on wildly,
virus, cell, and cloud.

Sleep is a book
the elders have written.
New limbs break through

mantles of old leaves.
I am a few leaves,
pressed in the book.

PREPARATORY MEDITATION

Edward Taylor

No preparation, no participation.
    Thomas Doolittle's *Treatise Concerning*
the Lord's Supper lies on Taylor's table,
        braced open next to pots of sugared teas,
        his writing tools, and cups of poultice-herbs
        to treat the ill parishioners come so

recently to Westfield and still beset
        with scurvy from poor provisions aboard
The Good Hope—or was it *Sanctity*? No
        matter. The detail's rich in the waiting.
        For now, the makings of a healing rub
        and sacks of apples, pale yams, though he fears

he needs a pinch more of Saint Johns-wort, as
        for each stomachic *Oyle of Spike most sweet*
May muskify thy Palace with their Reeke.
        How like a holding hand of God is his
        white antimonial cup, he thinks. How
        his grinding pestle's His Fury. His Club.

Every detail is prepared for conceit
        as for the mind prepared to wield it well.
This much he has taken from Sam. Sewall,

late Harvard roommate and Reverend High,
for whom *great Lightening and Three Claps of Loud
Thunder, the last very loud and startling,*

may betoken God's purposes, the strong
bolt like His Word, the Trinity peals
a providence, a portent, then presence . . .
Maybe Taylor's not as inflamed as Sam.;
yet his intelligence, his beacon
spirit, make him Increase Mather's chosen

shepherd for this Westfield flock, and here he
stays, and works for fifty-eight years, frontier
doctor-pastor-father. He sets aside
his papers to prepare more medicine—
as weekly he sets aside the sermon
to prepare the poem. *Not to prepare,*

he preaches then in sixteen ninety-three,
*is a Contempt of the Invitation;
and of the Wedden. It is to abide
in a Sordid, and filthy, wicked, and
Sinfull State. It is to abide without
the Wedden Garment, which is a right*

beautifull Garment. Huswifery is
a fitting figure to depict the true
alliance of God and all His peoples:

custody, service, and unending love.
    But enough. His visitors are soon due.
    The shepherd cannot minister the soul

unless the body is prepared as well,
    and everywhere's the temptation to fall
or fail. It may be *some sculking Rascals*
    in the woods, or weather's tribulation,
    or Man's own natural inclinations.
    Each substance is an image of each soul.

Hence all ore ugly, Nature Poysond stands,
    Lungs all Corrupted, Skin all botch't and scabd
A Feeble Voice, a Stinking Breath out fand
    And with a Scurfy Skale I'me all or clagd . . .
    Woe's mee. Undone! Undone! my Leprosy!
    Without a Miracle there is no Cure.

He hears the footfalls, then a soft knocking.
    His work will wait for his work to finish
—as his poems will lie packed, right, prepared
    for print until nineteen thirty-seven.
    When the sickly spirit comes beseeching,
    there is so little time to get ready.

THE RAINBOW

If things were worse, this cursed rain
would soak me unto sickness,
so Samuel Sewall might have
written in his vespers journal.
I have it on my writing desk
inside. For three days I have
labored with a saw and plane
and many boards to make my girl
a swingset near her mother's
lilac shrubs, as rain has drizzled
cold and meaningless. How
coherent was his world of works
and days, when *Plentifull Rains*
might connote a coming
providence—so Sewall notes
of Her Majesty's Court, June
the eighteenth, seventeen twelve.

> *We are well satisfyed with the Layin out*
> *of our Money—*

as on the same day clearly he
is mindful to remember that

Just before Sunset was a very NOBLE Rainbow,
one foot was between the Windmill, and the
Lazar house; other, on Dorchester Neck.

How faithful is the mind in
memory, connecting signs.
As the body of the Word
of God strides His world, so
Sam.'s determination to forge
meaning from his life's &c.
The day before, just this:

Great Heat, Much Rain.

Bulbs of lilac blooms burn like
black lights in the twilight. Rain
ascends in a mist where it has
fallen to the rich new grass.
It's Sunday, nearly dark, and
tomorrow I'm back in class to
shape my working days. I think
of him who keeps the task of church
and colony. He leans each night
long over paper waiting
on his writing desk. She can't wait,
my girl, to play on her swings.

Saw the New-raised meeting-house, 60. foot
long, 40. foot wide. Got to Cousin Woodbridge's
a little before Sunset. Saw an appearance of
a Rainbow-Colour about the bigness of a piece
of Timber one foot square and four foot long.
When I had turn'd from it, Somebody, call'd
to me to look on the Sight; and then it was
dilated like an Ensign with several bars in it.
Saw my daughter Judith.

It's what we connect. It's how
we join each thing with care. If I
soap a screw to drive it smoother,
if I run the ripsaw straight
against the wood grain down the meat
of my thumb, if the brackets hold,
if swivels keep the swings aligned,
it's because my father passed
a memory of such things to me.
Now I only work to make a toy.
My colleagues call that irony.
(Our meager making wants to
theorize each life we touch to death.)
If things were worse, I don't know if
I could make a living with my hands.
If things were worse than that, I could.

The Rainbow was very bright, and the Reflection
of it caused another faint Rainbow to the
westward of it. For the entire Compleateness
of it, throughout the whole Arch, and for its
duration, the like has been rarely seen. The
middle parts were discontinued for a while; but
the former Integrity and Splendor were quickly
Recovered. I hope this is a sure Token that
CHRIST Remembers his Covenant, and that He will
make haste to prepare for them a City that has
foundations, whose Builder and Maker is GOD.

My father circles in his
anger now. A stroke like lightning
shot his carotid artery one day.
He forgets himself. I'm worried
that my daughter may recall
my temper only, or my
little soul, my careless way
of cutting others down. The rage
for meaning makes us look for things
in other things, makes us hope
we see the future when we barely
see the day. I've beheld my girl
angry, impatient with the smallest
cause, cruel beyond her years.

Mrs. Sarah Banister, widow, dyes between 3
and 4 P.M., being drown'd with Dropsie.
News comes that Capt. Carver is Taken by two
Privateers. Just as had written this I went to look
of the Rain at my East-Chamber window, and
saw a perfect Rainbow. I think the setting of
the Sun caus'd its Disappearance. Laus Deo.

I put one good board beside
another and screw them down—so
things won't come apart, so she
won't fall. I think we wish too hard
for sense when what we want
is wonder, swinging on a toy.
I love the life we've made despite
our carelessness. I love the care.

Great rain with Thunder. Mr. Wadsworth
preaches: Work out your Salvation with Fear.

One night later, one more entry,
so Sewall becomes his vision.

Last night I dreamed that I had my daughter
Hirst in a little Closet to pray with her;
and of a sudden she was gon, I could not
tell how; although the Closet was so small,

and not Cumber'd with Chairs or Shelves,
I was much affected with it when I waked.

The mind is faithful in its
memory—connecting signs,
it makes a memory
to connect to what it needs.
The body will forget us all
anyway, in time, as it forgets
its breath, and how to live,
how to forgive. I keep this
story close whenever I grieve
or fear, growing cold. A father
and his child wait through a storm.
Great rain with Thunder. Fear has
drenched the child. (Is this my father,
or me, my girl, or someone
in a book? I don't remember.
Forgetfulness has taken part
of me already—besides,
it doesn't matter.) The child cries,
I'm scared, to which the father
whispers, holding on, Don't worry,
little one. I'll stay with you until
it's over. It's what he means by

Rainbow in the evening.

AFTER RAIN

1.

You have to turn your back to the animals.
      In theory it's better for them than shoes.
You have to hold them one leg at a time
      pinched with your legs to pick clean beneath each
hoof the sawdust, straw, mud-pack, pebbles, dung.
      The old ones stand patient while the young may
stomp the hard barn floor to tell you to quit
      or nod their long necks or quiver or huff.

2.

Rain has turned them skittish, the rain-flung leaves,
      whatever flies or crawls from a cold tree.
The scrape of your moon-crescent blade, as you
      carve each hoof hard as plastic or soft wood
down to the white heart, makes them want to grow
      wings, makes them want to fly or die or run.
You have to talk them down. Easy, you say
      in your own wind, soothing, easy now, whoa.

3.

But it's the long, continuous sighing
   breath of the file that stills them, for they know
you are through. You round the last edges down
   and smooth the hard breaks, as one by one they trot
through the tack room door, muscle, mane, shadow,
   turning their backs to you. Now the sun is out.
Barn swallows brighten the loft. You watch them
   break into flight, hoofprints filling with rain.

COLD WATER

Look at yourself, his soliloquy,
his sadness, while the others gather more
for their own solace than his. Then someone
offers to contact the authorities
and someone thinks to sit down——, someone hands
him a cup of cold water. It's snowing,
the sun blinks its searchlight through the snow, head-
lamp of a train and hit-and-run shadows,
though no one has hurt anyone here. Has
he been drinking? Did he OD? Was he
bumped in front of someone driving fast?
It's a gray swirl, the sidewalk, the stores—he
talks to the cup. He says *look at yourself.*
He takes a drink and everyone swallows.

TWO

These days are a great boon to men on the ground; the others are of changeable thunder, doomless, bringing nothing at all. Different persons praise different days, but few really know.

—Hesiod

POSTMODERNISM

The scene you loathe, the sheer fervor, the speed
    of the dangerous cabs—the city street
in oil, in spray when they pass, and the white
    exhaustion of the passersby like clouds.

You've been fired or you're on your way to work.
    If you're reading this, it doesn't matter.
What matters is you're wet, and hurrying
    or hungry, or not, or in no hurry

whatsoever. It's almost this easy.
    When you duck inside the cafe doorway,
the body smell of the animal stone,
    to find a little shelter, there's your face

like a face in the plate-glass sheet and door.
    There's the wealthy hungry seated inside.
On the other side, past the entrance, the rained-
    out passageway of air and stone, bombed-out

crapped-out building in a husk of smoke, there's
    the junkie, coughing on her cardboard flat.
You see because you see the reflection
    in the big glass, your face like an etching

between them, a breath, or a sudden change
     of venue. It's too convenient even
for art or argument—are you hungry?
          is she a junkie?—all of you framed for

an instant like a political ad.
     No one is looking at anyone else.
The street surges, it chokes, but you're caught there.
     And now even your pity is worthless.

DÉBUT DE SIÈCLE

underground 4 A.M.

No one on, no one off, no one around—
it's so late the train seems winded, blown in
on a pulse, pausing, the doorway bumping,
the eerie, warm, recirculating air
of the loading area like an oil.
The light's the hospital light where a death
or a baby is waiting behind walls.

Inside, pane on pane is glued over with
posters of perfume nudes, poetry slams,
jeremiads to family values
no one reads, no one is going to read.
It's a short ride to dawn and the new day.
Under your seat, a boot, old butts, ripped books.
By your head, two dots of semen on the glass.

DEJECTION

The sun is warm, the sky is clear,
    etc. . . . Quickly he taps
a full nib twice to the mouth of
    his japan-ink bowl—harder than
    he had thought, if he had thought—smears
the fine spattering with his sleeve,
    and continues, for whom haste is
more purity than certainty,
as *anarchy is better than despotism*—

for this reason—that the former
    is for a season & that the
latter is eternal. These days
    have been quickened with sightseeing,
    Mary and Claire at Virgil's tomb,
the Bay of Baiae, until poor health
    overtakes Shelley descending
Vesuvius by torch light, who
collapses with agonizing pain in his side.

Now his chamber is rebellion
    enough. He bears down, scratching lines
on the back of the stanzas he
    will later discard: "My head is wild
    with weeping!" Famous among friends

for his sloth, as for his passions,
 he once lived in a room described
by Mr. Thomas Jefferson
Hogg, thus: *Books, boots, papers, shoes, philosophical*

 instruments, clothes, pistols, linen,
  crockery, ammunition, and
 phials innumerable, with
  money, stockings, prints, crucibles,
  bags, and boxes in every place . . .
 The tables, and especially
  the carpets, were already stained
 with large spots of various hues,
which frequently proclaimed the agency of fire.

 Alas! I have not hope nor health,
  Nor peace within, etc. . . .
 We lived in utter solitude,
  Mary writes in her journal of
 the days. Still, Pompeii staggers him,
and its distant, deep peals rattle
  like subterranean thunder
beneath the family's lodging rooms.
The lightning of the noontide ocean is flashing

 around me, etc. . . . How
  might Prometheus consider
 these ruins, surrounding, the rooms
  a shamble, and the posthumous

greatness of the Greeks more theory
than presence? Yet theories abound.

For all their visionary zeal,
the pamphlets and tracts, sheer brilliance
of his *Defence,* and hope, he is characterized

more seditious than inspiring.
John Coleridge, Samuel's nephew:
Mr Shelley would abrogate
*   our laws—this would put an end to*
*   felonies and misdemenours . . .*
he would abolish the rights of
*   property, he would overthrow*
the constitution . . . no army
or navy; he would pull down our churches, level

the Establishment. This is at
*   least intelligible; but it*
is not so easy to describe
*   the structure, which Mr Shelley*
*   would build upon this vast heap of*
ruins. 'Love', he says, 'is the sole law
*   which shall govern the moral world'.*
The great gift, foresight, produces
foes instead of a god. His fingers blaze with ink.

For I am one whom men love not,
    etc. . . . His friend Southey:

With all his genius, he was a
   base, bad man. Carlyle is plainer:
   He is a poor, thin, spasmodic,
hectic, shrill, and pallid being.
   Tomorrow will bring a tour of
Naples, and better spirits, and
peace with Mary and Claire. He is just twenty-six—

all his life lies ahead. The bay
   burns wild beyond his window
in holy admixtures of fire
   and water . . . the grand effusion
   symbolic but real to him
as well. The boats are running far
   and fast. He wonders whether he
might take time to charter one, sail
the Elysian Fields, the Caverns of the Sibyl . . .

He fills his pen. He must hurry.
   The fires of new thought swell in his
hand like a torch. Tomorrow,
   the sea, into which he will peer
   —so translucent that you could see
the hollow caverns clothed with the
   glaucous sea-moss, & the leaves, &
branches of those delicate weeds
that pave the unequal bottom of the water.

SEPARATION

1.

Twice you have driven nearly off the road.
But you're making a mile a minute, less
the headwind, less the time it takes to stop
for fuel or food or stretch at a truckstop.
It's ten, it's midnight—then it's three-thirty.
Little towns constellate in the great black
field, connected, clarified, and on line
with the line your headlamps draw. You're tracing
a myth, you're drawing your longbow back, stick
figure of phone poles and train-trestle posts
racing unwinded beside you, one gold
light far in a field as a firefly, fire—.
When you come to a stop at the crossroads,
the little town-square cannon aims above you
through the trees. And when you've gone through
the last lights again, into the darkness,
you see the steady gold of the field light
waver, now, grown larger, winded, ablaze.

2.

It's a fire, feral in the wind, whipping
high the tips of the elder trees, flames in
flares shooting, the roaring heat a cloud. It's
a whole house gone up or barn or back building.
You're awake, slowing, rolling your window.
The one you have left has left your dreaming.
But the crowd in attendance is past worrying—
they wait, or warm themselves, something tribal
in their tribulation the way they stand
relaxed beside the trucks, choking smoke, or
bend at the waist to drink from the buckets.
Smell of old wood, highway speed, gasoline—.
But then you have passed them. The thin blue ink
of your lamps scrawls ahead to the blackness,
nothing but night and sky and the time it
takes to drive all night. There is nothing else
but stars and star-stories, which, like your heart,
are clearer the greater grows the darkness.

"FADE-OUT": A LOVER'S DISCOURSE

This photograph of fog
the small clearing gives up

to a late winter sky,
gray gauze of exhaustion,

we do not know who is
speaking; the text speaks,

that is all: no more
image, nothing but language.

the day above freezing
for the first time in weeks . . .

she has left it here
for me to find, the way

Like a kind of melancholy
mirage, the other withdraws

into infinity, and I wear myself
out trying to get there.

In the text the fade-out
of voices is a good thing;

the voices of the narrative
come, go, disappear, overlap;

this heat of old snows
suddenly melting,

or not-melting, but
given off as emanation,

But the other is not a text,
the other is an image,

if the voice is lost, it is
the entire image which vanishes.

the background trees,
the high bleached sycamores

ruined in snow-grain, hold
the fog, will not let go.

It is her way of saying
without saying what we know.

She was alone in the house.
She went to these woods.

which will be swallowed up
far away by cold depths:

such a voice is 'about'
to vanish, as the exhausted

This was before we
had exhausted ourselves

of ourselves. It freezes me
to think of such care—

alarmed by everything which
appears to alter the image.

I am, therefore, alarmed
by the other's fatigue:

as though she has gone there
and not come back,

as though she is background,
a granular, fierce fog

Nothing is more lacerating
than a voice at once beloved

and exhausted . . . a voice
from the end of the world,

Later, she lifted print
after print to light,

the fog of each photograph
scaling gray to a cloud.

being is 'about' to die:
fatigue is infinity:

what never manages
to end. I am

to break through woods,
out of haze, backwards,

footprint by print, so
her path fades into trees

It is the cruelest
of all rival objects.

How combat exhaustion?
I can see that the other,

exhausted, tears off
a fragment of this fatigue

in order to give it to me.
But what am I to do

and not-here, and not there.
Now she steps backwards

out of bare trees, through
the snow, and now back

'Take care of me?'
No one answers, for what

is given is precisely
'what does not answer.'

the heat of piled snow
cedes to the limbs.

Once more I find her desire,
to be doubled, to be here

with this bundle of fatigue
set down before me?

What does this gift mean?
'Leave me alone?'

into the fog of the trees.
She has left the picture

for me to hold. She is fog
given up to the trees.

SIMONIDES' STONE

1.

I'm trippin' I'm trippin' could be his song if
his circumstance weren't song's opposite or his
voice more than one note of despair. He's sitting
on steep stairs leading

to a gated brownstone. There's almost nothing
left of him, no shoulders in the service coat,
no ears beneath the hair, no shoes, and the group
of kids shooting hoops,

passing a stub pipe of something unlit, doesn't
notice until the song gets louder and he
shifts, then cries out *fuckin' trippin'*—then settles
down and seems to sleep.

Man's strength is little, and futile his concerns,
his lifespan short, filled with trouble, and over
it death, inescapable, uniform, looms to
high and low alike.

2.

Which is how Simonides made his wage. This
is "the first poetry about which we can
say, these are texts written to be read: literature,"
so notes Anne Carson

of Simonides' practice, paid in plenty,
of carving verse epitaphs onto stone (it's
the fifth century B.C.) in elegy,
paean, victory, grief.

He tapped his chisel lightly. He lined his words
horizontally as well as vertically,
shaping them into grids "like ranks of men in
military form——."

"Only an inscriptional poet has to
measure his inspiration against the size
of his writing surface," thus Simonides
"counting out letters,

3.

cutting away space, reckoning prices . . ." Puff
of dust. A verse.

The kids are spray painting the
entrance to the alley with their names, their tags,
swirling shadow-marks,

meaning it's their neighborhood, stay out or die.
They paint the handrail leading down some steps where
people sleep on cardboard after dark. They rap
a song, a rhyme, no

time to live, no time to die: one dances off
with a can until the others chase him back.
They are laughing and then they are not. They stop
where the man's bedded

down, stone-cold, covered in leaves. They paint the stairs.
They spray some thick, blue lines and shadow them with
red around his form. They do not write on him.
Man's dirge is praise.

TO WINTER

The poetry of earth
     is never dead.
It flies down, white wind, whipped,
     a swirling snow—
white sound. It's what you hear
     this side of sleep.
One whole side of the house
     seems hurt with it.

And when will you rest who've
     stayed awake for
days, in illness, white woe . . .
     Even the stripped
pines are an order of
     sleep, the way they
hurt from the shoulder-weight
     of snow, crack, and

fall, their downed limbs blown white.
     Even the wind—.
In the city last week
     you watched the young
beggars, some coins pitched in
     a plate, holding

hands, hold on. Whatever
        they were to each

other, intimate, poor
        relation, a
poor fraud, as passersby
        uttered, *hooker*
or *heroin head,* the
        song they offered
was a kind of poetry,
        a kind of sleep

for a soul, if beyond
        measure, fatigued.
And when will deliverance
        be given, in
recompense for our pain . . .
        —and in what coin?
The fallen snow lay humped
        as souls asleep

in doorways, beside curbs,
        as it falls now
and settles, as the blood
        settles in its
own strict poverty. Of
        the white tide
like a vast wind, viral,
        cellular with

snowfall, of a sea blown
      silver rich with
its own fierce destruction,
      Keats feared he gazed
too far through it, as here,
      where every maw
the greater on the less
      feeds evermore.

You watch the days and nights
      in a blinking
eye pass. Ice, wind, snow, white
      wave on wave—the
pine boughs slapped with it—what
      can you offer
but yourself? So the snow
      falls down, like

foliage, and the poet
      puts words away.
Let the poor in spirit
      freeze where they have
gathered at our feet, and
      let the sleeping
begin. The earth knows. Wind—.
      Here follows prose.

THE CITY OF GOD

Now we knelt beside
the ruined waters
as our first blood,
our bulb-before-bloom,
unfurled too early

in slender petals.
Now we were empty.
Now we walked for months
on softer shoes and
spoke, not quite with grief.

This morning four deer
come up to the yard
to stand, to be stunned,
at the woods' edge
on their hoof-tips. Their

ears twist like tuners,
but they stay for minutes,
minutes more, while
we are shadows behind
windows watching them

nip at the pine bark,
nibble some brown tips
of hydrangea. It's
been a mean, dry winter.
The last time I prayed—

prayed with any thought
of reply, any
hope of audience—
I sat in a church
and the city smell

of lilac, fumes from
the bus line, filled me.
The joys of the body
are not the sins
of the soul.

       Who knows
how many have come
to be with us? We
knelt, not as in prayer,
beside the toilet

and watched the first one
leave us utterly—.
They were deer. Now they
are fog.
       Now the wind

pulls back though the trees.
We know it will
be this way always
—whatever fades—
and the dreadful wake.

THE PURITAN WAY OF DEATH

How hard this life is hallowed by the body.
How burdened the ground where they have hollowed it,
     where they have gathered to set the body back,

handful by handful, the broken earth of her.
They have gathered to sift back the broken clod
     of her body, to settle her, now, back down.

"A child is a man in a small letter,"wrote
John Earle in sixteen twenty-eight,"Natures fresh
     picture newly drawne in Oyle, which Time and much

handling dimmes and defaces," wrote Prof. David
E. Stannard, Yale, nineteen seventy-seven.
     A stutter of winter wind shakes the plane trees

until they seem, leafless, huddled over, to weep.
But John Earle was not a Puritan. Here then,
     at the grave of the girl who was sorely bitten

by the Small Pox, they do not bow down, neither
raise their heads nor hold hands against the cold.
     This fruit of natural corruption and root

of actual rebellion both against God
and man must be destroyed, and no manner of
         way nourished . . . For the beating, and keeping down

of this stubbornness parents must provide
carefully, instructed John Robinson in
         the same year as Earle's *Micro-cosmographie.*

The frozen ground of their gaze steadies them.
The gray grasses shiver and snap at their feet.
         They do what they can. Long days and nights they stand

with her, through her fevers and ague, and clean her
gentle Vomit, and try to soothe the Pustules
         and her Eruptions, until there grow Hundreds,

and neither then a common poultice of Lint
dipt in the Variolous Matter, nor warmed
         Leaves of the Cabbage laid to her rapid heart,

nor prodigious bleeding, nor prayer, can save her.
They go astray as soon as they are born. They
         no sooner step *than they* stray, *they no sooner*

lisp *than they* ly, mourns Cotton Mather, sixteen
eighty-nine. Yet he himself is father to
         fifteen, and loves them, suffering their afflictions.

He sees in his *Lambs* in the *Fold* evidence
of God's love. Moreso His fury. *Are they* Young?
        Yet the Devil *has been with them already.*

At least, let us give thanks for a lease so short
that terror has short time to dwell. Only two
        of Mather's children live beyond their father,

as though a father's fealty be his children.
So the lamplighter takes up his grim vigil,
        torch in hand, and together we walk the slick path

through the centuries, where the ministers shall
say what has been said, what needs be repeated.
        Oh, blood upon the hands. Urine to the lips.

Let us burn the garments of disease lest they
cloak us now, and let our faith be provender,
        provision, and protection, and offer no

ly, no calumny, nor any words but these.
Let us stand before the door and gaze outward.
        Field and fallow. Fish and fowl. Mall and highway

now alike. She lives among us——. *She is ours,*
flesh of our flesh, whom our sorrows have begot.
        Let us walk beside ourselves with this grief, who

neither raise our heads nor hold hands to the cold.

She goes beside us, even so, even as

      I write this to you, neighbor, friend, daughter,

my reader, this day, in nineteen ninety-nine.

She reminds us always of this death, this life,

      which is redundant, awful, endless, and ours.

THREE

And so the year turns over and over on itself,
Traces the tracks it has laid many times before . . .

—Proba

UNCONDITIONAL ELECTION

We have decided now to kill the doves
—November the third, nineteen ninety-nine—
who gather in great numbers in the fields
of Ohio, vast and diminishing,

whose call is gray and cream, wing-on-the-wind.
I lean from the deck to hear their mourning
cry, like the coo of a human union.
They persevere as song in the last days.

Or is it the wind I hear this morning,
crossing the great, cold lake, the hundred dry
miles of fields cut down to stubble and rust?
The rain gauge, hollow as a finger bone,

lifts to survey the stiffening breeze.
The boards of our deck are a plank bridge
hanging over nothing, the season's abyss.
When we decided not to have the child,

how could we know the judgment would carry
so far?—each breath, each day, another
renewal of our *no*. A few frail leaves
hurry now dryly in waves at my feet.

The doves have no natural predator,
so we will be their fate. We will prowl
the brown fields, taking aim at the wind,
or huddle inside in the lengthening dark.

It no longer matters who is right. Their cry
comes from both sides of the window at once.

MIDWEST: ODE

in memoriam William Matthews

You could believe a life so plain it means
calmness in the lives of others, who come
to see it, hold it, buy it piece by piece,
as these good people easing from their van
onto the curb where the big-shoed children
of Charm, Ohio, have lined their baskets
of sweet corn, peaches, and green beans.
Each Saturday morning the meeting point
of many worlds is a market in Charm.

You could believe a name so innocent
it is accurate and without one blade
of irony, and green grass everywhere.
Yet, how human a pleasure the silk hairs
when the corn is peeled back, and the moist worm
curls on the point of an ear like a tongue—
how charged the desire of the children who
want to touch it, taste it, turn it over,
until it has twirled away in the dust.

There are black buggies piled high with fruit pies.
There are field things hand-wrought of applewood
and oak, and oiled at the palm of one man.
There are piecework quilts black-striped and maroon

and mute as dusk, and tatting, and snow shawls,
and cozies the colors of prize chickens—
though the corporate farm five miles away
has made its means of poultry production
faster, makes fatter hens, who need no sleep,

so machinery rumbles the nights through.
Still, it is hard to tell who lives with
more placid curiosity than these,
not only the bearded men in mud boots
and city kids tugging on a goat rope,
but really the whole strange market of Charm,
Ohio, where weekly we come, who stare
and smile at each other, to weigh the short
business end of a dollar in our hands.

THAT MOON

1.

They are halfway
between here
      and dying,
      our Canada geese,

as this evening
we pick down
      the pine path.
      They are so hungry,

landing, they howl
as rowdy
      as birddogs.
      First they're a dozen

gathering on
the lake muck
      where we go—
      then more melting down,

wide on their wings,
wild from the

flight, hitting
hard, flat stone, splashing.

Each night now we
have walked down
        to watch them,
        Katie and I, as

though we are part
of the phase,
        seasonal
        chill, migratory:

and so we are,
hand in hand.
        They're so big!
        like her voice scaring

a couple up
among pine
        pollen clouds,
        moon past its midphase,

those long black wings
whipping a
        little wind-
        rotor that whirrs

out and above
the flint creek.
     Now she's still.
     Now everything stills.

Only, not those
green whisker-
     thin tubes of
     wild onion grasses

slick on the slope
at our feet,
     nor black moss
     tightening its last

shadow against
pin oaks, pines,
     flat granite
     shelving, nor the wind

everywhere—we
watch the geese
     a moment
     longer—nor that moon

sliver, silvering
over with

haze. There is
another story.

2.

In the house of
the grown child
      —listen, Kate—
      from their last, short time

together, each
morning finds
      the remnant
      melting more, one piece

of shower soap . . .
that landscape.
      That loss, too—
      soft stone, slow as clock-

work—left behind
from his last
      visit, the
      father, dead these weeks

darkening down.
Soggy, shape

of a curled
finger, caked, cracking,

it weeps away
and no one
    will take it
    out, move it along,

nor use it, as
it beggars
    use. Color
    of the leaving moon. That

moon. Listen, more
are coming,
    little heart—
    new dew like lotion.

The geese find their
loud way down
    to us, whose
    breath is visible

(invisible)
as black wings.
    Nothing stays
    still. The new moon, no

moon night's just a
few steps off.
      Look now how
      our Canadas are

settling down, though
more alight,
      land, drink, tuck
      their beaks beneath their

big wings for rest.
And that moon
      we come for
      —watch your step—it's a

rib, now, crescent,
your father's
      eyelash. And
      soon the night entire.

MIDWEST: GEORGICS

1.

The wind is the weather. The worst will blow
off the surge in a matter of moments—
the best is a blessing, less rain or ruin
but no less a shock for the suddenness.
In the time it takes the wind to turn, or
a voice to turn into wind, we have gone
from the hulking balers to box lots lined
on long tables, books and bruised silver, out-
landish toys, tools, strange clothes, crates of nothings.
It's a bright day in a killer summer
and we're kicking through a wasted bean field,
trying to pick up, on a slow thermal,
the near-harmonic of twin auctioneers
setting the price for farm things from on high.

2.

I wish I were like the famous poet
—disembodied, a voice out of nowhere—
postmodern and uninvolved. *What I am
trying to get at is a general,*

all-purpose experience—like those stretch
socks that fit all sizes. The particular
occasion is of lesser interest
to me than the way a happening or
experience filters through me. Words flit
by with the force of fate, missed. A gray gull
coasts off on a costly breeze—then calls back
over one wing, unintelligible
as a critic, foundling, fond . . . *it sounds like*
nobody's story in particular.

3.

And that would be fine, except here we are,
come for the auction of a neighbor's dead
farm, flooded, snowed out, burned out by drought
and years of subsidy undercosting,
another neighbor . . . in particular:
Thom. Dawson, his wife Rachel, their son, Sam,
in their particular death-throe, blown down
utterly by their bank, itself an arm
of a swollen corporate torso. Look
at them leaning on air. It's worse than
a wake. The ones being mourned attend their
own ceremony, selling-off of goods
and souls, and three mouths to feed. Such pain is
serious, tangible, unironic . . .

4.

Look at them leaning in plaid shirts and boots.
Will one pair of socks keep their six feet dry?
Shoppers! Friends! Neighbors! Let us consider
the values at hand! And let's help our friends—
this could happen to you, too, anytime.
What am I bid for—and across the green
back yard, cut into dumpy subplots by
massive four-wheelers, rented U-Hauls, like
an argument echoing, the other
gaunt crier holds up a desk lamp, clicks it
on to prove it still works—*Who'll give me five*
bucks? They're the gods hereabouts, who call down
the best price, brother-barkers, Jim-'n-I
Auctioneers (no kidding), in much demand.

5.

My autobiography has never
interested me very much. Whenever
I try to think about it, I seem to
draw a complete blank. The poet's sales rep:
All that is needed is for the reader
to be within range of the poem to
experience its beneficial effects.
There floats a reek of cattle on a breeze

from the gone barn—lilac and acid, sharp
as a pinch to the nose—and a shift in
the cheap wind twists the voices about, out
of their heads, meaningless as merchandise.
The crowd turns to vapor, dust, cloud. A draft
off the lake tosses a gull like a cup.

6.

Think of a place the gods have forsaken
and bathe it in sunshine and water. That's
the fate of the farmhouse and fields, foreclosed
by bad fencing, big pickups. *Bad weather,*
as we say, *bad as it comes,* when what we
mean is luck, money, love: anything but
ash, berry-brambles, the trash when we've gone.
I wish we could all be like the poet,
out-of-body, misrepresentative
of our bad luck and lot, no one's story.
But this is what it means to have our life.
It means wanting to fly off on each wind.
It means living among neighbors but cursing
the gods, who talk down to us on sheer air.

WORKS AND DAYS

More in number, five
or six at a time
perched atop stiff cat-

tail tufts or calling
from lush caverns in
the willow limbs—more

on the wing, more flash
and blood, more wild song,
who seldom travel

in numbers bigger
than a pair—the red-
wings returning this

spring to the park pond
have surprised us all.
It's supposed to be

a bad time for birds.
El Nino has smeared
California

for months, spreading east
and windward its strain
of killer drought, of

greenhouse-effect storms.
A few blocks away
the factory mill

dusts our own fields with
a mineral mist—
pesticide spills from

the well-water taps.
The honeybees are
dying out and what-

ever food these birds
are used to has thinned
next to nothing: yet

here they are, bright as
bobbers, floating the
rich, brown surfaces.

It's a windless day
of someone's childhood.
Small wonder so many

of us have come
to sun with the red-
wings on the flat bank.

The birds, to see us,
must think all is well,
to see so many

so happy to be
here——, to see so many
more gathering now.

MR. WHITMAN'S BOOK

The trouble is drink, if like fate drink is
not a destination but destiny—
Franklin the orphan, Franklin the fast thief,
Franklin, on a terrible binge, marries
the mulatto, Margaret, who murders
a rival and then kills herself in prison.
The story is so good it tells itself.

It's autumn, eighteen forty-two, and New
York is electric, emergent, wealthy—
a place for a greenhorn printer pamphleteer
to find energy to drive his Great Book.
He writes without stopping, stopping only
to stroll the Bowery running with dock boys
and street-whores, or take his cup with the wags

of Tammany, basking in their rank yarns.
In three days he will finish—as he claims
for decades—three days without sleep, three days
and help of a bottle of port, *or what not,*
and *Franklin Evans* is so scandalous
it sells out the next week, twenty-thousand-
plus copies, the novel the whole number

of *New World,* November the twenty-third,
at twelve-and-a-half cents a fresh issue.
Franklin the con, Franklin inebriate,
sleeping in the purlieus of the markets,
or on the docks—sometimes, going for two days
with hardly a morsel of food. I managed
to get liquor by one means or another . . .

Yet how sad the book, unsigned, signed only
"By a Popular American Author,"
becomes his life's best-seller, wild with mass
appeal, when the later Leaves will be stamped,
signed, photographed with so much Self, and self-
reviewed in four newspapers, but barely read.
Still, who touches this book touches a man.

In another version, this from J. G.
Schumaker, journalist friend of the Author,
it's *gin-cocktails,* not port, keep him going,
sweating in a reading room near Tammany.
(Book and man are indistinguishable
to the Amherst muse, too, *little tippler*
and half fiction herself, who never read

his Book—but was told he was disgraceful—.)
Disgrace drives straight to the heart. *I sicken*
as I narrate this part of my story,
Franklin tells us, who has walked madly and

swiftly through the streets, aching in gas light,
until he finds Colby at a tavern,
and might have added *murder* to his crimes

had bystanders not pulled him off in time.
Yet it's Franklin the convert whose reform
describes the circle of the narrative,
Franklin the temperate, Franklin the found,
for whom self-salvation is a model
of Progress. His piety is stylized
as street-talk one instant, sermon the next.

Mercy and charity should be ever
present in our minds!—he cries out so—
for none can know, but they who have felt it—
the burning, withering thirst for drink!
The Washingtonians have spread their sway
up the Eastern seaboard, their temperance
and clout, their bullying for elections,

and it's clear the author seeks to appeal
to their melodramatic cleanliness.
Clear, too, his own hope for conversion.
The fervent Leaves unfold with its promise,
political, natural, sexual,
holy, all alike endear'd, and dating
back undoubtedly to his primal shame,

eighteen forty, his secret, the "almost
tragedy" at Woodbury—rumors that
run him from town, some kind of trouble with
boy-pupils, their parents, feathers and tar . . .
Thus planted, his impulse to correct,
to reform his own cravings and disgrace,
and thereby ours. The third account, this from

Mr. Eldridge, reports relays of strong
whiskey cocktails, which keep the printer's devil,
who was waiting, supplied with copy equal
to anything in the Book of Genesis.
Whitman the vulgate, Whitman self-sainted.
Even Hopkins touches it, who knows in
his heart Walt Whitman's mind to be more like

his own than any other man's living.
As he is a very great scoundrel this
is not a very pleasant confession.
So much for Franklin. So much for trouble—
though the Author foretells, *if my story*
meets with that favor which writers are
perhaps too fond of relying upon,

my readers may hear from me again.
Soon the insurgence, and Leaves, soon the War
and Lincoln and the legions dead, wounded,
wondering what happened to the promise

of perfection. Soon now the sweet old man
of Mickle Street, the strokes and lectures, wrapped
in a shawl, hardly stirring for the pain

of tubercules, awash still with Visions
from his improvised waterbed. The street
clamors—his readers now coming to call—
Traubel the nursemaid, Traubel the doorman,
Traubel the scribe, saying *Mr. Harned*
has brought us all two bottles of sweet port.
But the hero will not touch his all night.

HUMBLE HOUSE

Even the lawn is cramped with hydrangeas,
white heirloom lilies, wild creeper roses
running the length of the porch, all of it
sloped on a grade from the yard to the road.

The perspective is childhood or old age,
poor, but not poor enough to discern it.
Nor is the house large enough to waste room.
Perhaps company will come soon, unannounced—

but no one will sit in the sitting room.
That's for Hummel figurines, for small frames
unpolished for months, tarnished as flatware,
for old plates, photos, plastic-covered chairs.

That's for the passing of the spirit world
through the spirit of the house. Everyone
would rather stand in the kitchen where fruit
pies crisp on the sill, swing on the side porch,

or sit smoking or sewing or talking,
or take coffee in a cane chair upstairs.
There's a functional humility in
everything but that room, where nobody stays.

Soon enough we will go to our places
down the road, where the creek cuts through the graves.
The whole family waits there, passing toward home,
worm and mole, creeper and clod, humus, loam.

OHIO FIELDS AFTER RAIN

The slow humped backs of ice ceased
to shadow the savannahs of Ohio millennia
ago, right where we've sailed to a stop.
The shaken woman leaves open her car door
and familiar as relatives we touch hands
in the middle of the wet, black road.
To the north new corn enriches by the hour.

South of us—really, just over a fence—
heavy boulders rolled thousands of miles
quit the migration and grew down,
huddled, cropped, scarred by the journey.
"I couldn't," she says, "stop skidding,"
and I know what she means, having
felt the weight of my car planing a scant

millimeter over the highway glaze. Calmly
she slid to one shoulder, I to the other,
and the earth spun onward without us.
What a place we have come to, scooped
hollow of hillsides, cut valleys, drumlins
and plains. And where the rain settles,
the gray beasts growing tame on the shore.

TWO CLOUDS

for Ann

      White mist burns
like the wings
of egrets,
unfolding
in new light.

      White mist lifts,
and the gray
mist of rain
floats through it.
Is it three,

> *out of this*
> *veil of mist*
> *lifts a sail*   —Gakoku

      is it four
days now we've
stayed inside?
Storms have raged
and pursued,

      the gutters
have gone wild

with pinecones—
is it mice
dashing their

    claws all rain
long, up, down?
We have loved
and listened
as our house

    has settled
into its
storm rhythm,
the breathing
between rooms,

    the dust, pine
pollen, wind
on the panes,
the sump-pump
deep in our

    dirt basement
rinsing out
like a pulse
the rising
quick waters,

which would chew
away our
foundation.
How strange: how
familiar

the soft click
far below,
the on/off
throb we don't
hear until,

heard, it is
all we hear.
Is this the
same dreamy
reverie

clouds come from
time to time—
chance to rest   —Basho

of the man
who lay for
weeks, haunted
by his heart?—
Barney Clark,

who couldn't
live without
Jarvik's art-
ificial
pump, yet who

couldn't rest
with it, the
wash of blood
a motor
more steady

than any
body. "It's
not dying,"
our neighbor
says, hospice

nurse, old friend.
"It's waiting . . .
not knowing"—
this, after
your reading

at the book-
store, sober,
elegiac,
poems full
of the dead,

the landscape
of mourning.
"I could hang
by my hair
for three years

　　　if I knew
it would be
three years! The
waiting—that's
what you need

　　　to write your
poems about."
What a strange
rhythm has
marriage, long

　　　　　　　　　. . . why not
　　　　　　　　　be alone
　　　　　　　　　together?　　—Moore

　　　privacy
learned in grief
and laughter,
as now, as
you float on

our bed's white
clouds, asleep
or serene.
How I love
you again

and again,
wave on wave,
like rain, now
the bright sun,
and still how

easy it
becomes to
wash over
the daily
inflictions,

the subtle,
uncertain
damages
running the
length of

one's loving.
Waiting is
what we do
together,
beautifully,

        deepening—
your hair on
my hand, my
heart in yours.
Who knows when

                                    winds that blow,
                                    which leaf is
                                    next to go?   —Soseki

        it will end?
The long rain,
the white mist
going up
so slowly.

        I don't know,
and it lifts me.

92

NOTES

I have aspired in this book to the ventriloquist's art—borrowings, hauntings, quotations, and citations throughout. Some of the broader applications of others' work is as follows:

"Romanticism": Emerson's account of his first wife Ellen's illness is taken from a letter on the day of her death, February 9, 1832, to his Aunt Mary. His brother Charles wrote, in a letter to another brother, William, that Waldo was "as one over whom the waters have gone." On March 29, Emerson entered this solitary sentence in his journal: "I visited Ellen's tomb & opened the coffin." The comments about dreams, beasts, and keys are also from his journals.

"Preparatory Meditation": From 1682 until his retirement in 1725, the pastor of the Congregational Church of Westfield, Massachusetts, Rev. Edward Taylor, wrote two long series of poems which he entitled *Preparatory Meditations before my Approach to the Lords Supper. Chiefly upon the Doctrin preached upon the Day of administration.* Taylor wrote at least 195 of these poems in order to prepare himself to administer and receive the sacrament of the Lord's Supper on certain Sundays. I have quoted lines from his "Meditation 27. Upon Deb. 9.13.14. How much more shall the Blood of Christ etc." of the second series, and have borrowed from other poems and sermons. I have used the stanza form (but not the rhyme) he developed for these meditations. Written for himself and packed away for more than two centuries, Edward Taylor's poetry did not appear in print until 1937, when Thomas H. Johnson gathered and published a selection of them. The passage from Sewall is from *The Diary of Samuel Sewall*.

"The Rainbow": Despite the fury and indictment in his public tracts and sermons, the American Puritan minister Samuel Sewall could be tender, confessional, even self-doubting in his nightly diary, which he kept from 1673 until three months before his death in 1729. No detail was too small for Sewall's attentions, since any occurrence might yield God's intents and purposes. Even the weather, one of Sewall's favorite notations, was a holy language to be read by devout souls.

"Dejection": This poem takes its stanza and syllabic form from Shelley's ode, "Stanzas, written in dejection, near Naples." I have incorporated several short passages from his poem into mine, and I have also borrowed fragments from *The Letters of Percy Bysshe Shelley*. The passage from Thomas Jefferson Hogg comes from his early biography, *The Life of Percy Bysshe Shelley*, while Mary Shelley's sentence is taken from *Mary Shelley's Journal*. John Taylor Coleridge's remarks are from an article he published in 1819 in *Quarterly Review*. I found the remarks by Robert Southey and Thomas Carlyle in Isabel Quigly's introduction to Penguin Poetry Library's *Shelley: Selected Poems*.

"'Fade-Out': A Lover's Discourse": The italicized stanzas (footprints, accompaniments) are from Roland Barthes's alphabetic prose work, *A Lover's Discourse*.

"Simonides' Stone": Though I have relined it, the passage from Simonides' poem is M. L. West's translation. Anne Carson's commentary comes from her *Economy of the Unlost: Reading Simonides of Keos with Paul Celan*.

"To Winter": I have used a few phrases from two of Keats's poems, his epistolary piece "To J. H. Reynolds Esq." and "On the Grasshopper and Cricket."

"The Puritan Way of Death": I am indebted to David E. Stannard, whose *The Puritan Way of Death: A Study in Religion, Culture, and Social Change* provided many useful details and passages for my poem. The method of treatment for smallpox is taken from Zabdiel Boylston's *The Way of Proceeding in the Small Pox Inoculated in New England,* published in 1721 and probably written in collaboration with Cotton Mather. Mather's own comments come from his 1689 tract, *Small Offers Towards the Service of this Tabernacle in this Wilderness.* The passage from John Robinson is from his *New Essays: Or, Observations Divine and Moral;* John Earle's is from his *Microcosmographie or, A Piece of the World Discovered in Essays and Characters.* Both of these books were published in 1628.

"Mr. Whitman's Book": Whitman wrote and published a considerable body of fiction (as well as traditional verse) in the 1840s. His longest work of fiction is a temperance novel first advertised as *Franklin Evans, or The Inebriate: A Tale of the Times.—By a Popular American Author,* and printed on November 23rd, 1842, in the weekly New York magazine *New World* as a special "Extra" edition in octavo. I have borrowed passages from this novel as well as phrases from "Song of Myself."

When asked by her literary advisor, Thomas Wentworth Higginson, whether she was familiar with Whitman's poetry, Emily Dickinson replied to him in a letter in 1862: "You speak of Mr Whitman—I never read his Book—but was told that he was disgraceful—." Gerard Manley Hopkins's equally cautious comment comes from his letter of October 18, 1882, to his friend, the poet Robert Bridges.

"Two Clouds": The small poems running down the right-hand panel of this poem are my tri-syllabic renderings of Harold G. Henderson's translations of haiku. The Marianne Moore passage is from "Marriage."

ABOUT THE AUTHOR

David Baker is the author of five previous books of poems: *The Truth about Small Towns* (1998), *After the Reunion* (1994), *Sweet Home, Saturday Night* (1991), *Haunts* (1985), and *Laws of the Land* (1981). His two books of criticism are *Heresy and the Ideal: On Contemporary Poetry* (2000) and *Meter in English: A Critical Engagement* (1996). Among his awards are fellowships and prizes from the National Endowment for the Arts, John Simon Guggenheim Memorial Foundation, Ohio Arts Council, Society of Midland Authors, Poetry Society of America, and the Pushcart Foundation. His poems and essays appear in such magazines as *The Atlantic Monthly, DoubleTake, The Nation, The New Republic, The New Yorker, The Paris Review, Poetry,* and many others. Baker was raised in Missouri and currently resides in Granville, Ohio, where he serves as poetry editor of *The Kenyon Review*. He teaches at Denison University and in the M.F.A. program for writers at Warren Wilson College.